22.79

Walkingsticks

Walkingsticks

Patrick Merrick

THE CHILD'S WORLD®, INC.

Library of Congress Cataloging-in-Publication Data
Merrick, Patrick.
Walkingsticks/Patrick Merrick.
P.   cm.
Includes index.
Summary: Describes the physical characteristics, habitat, behavior, and life cycle
of the insect called the walkingstick.
ISBN 1-56766-383-4 (lib. bdg.)
1. Stick insects—Juvenile literature. [1. Stick insects.]
I. Title.
QL509.5.M47   1997
595.7'29—dc21   96-46957
CIP
AC

Photo Credits

COMSTOCK/Gwen Fidler: 29
DPA/DEMBINSKY PHOTO ASSOC: 23, 30
Joe McDonald: 2, 9, 10, 13
Robert and Linda Mitchell: 16, 24, 26
Art Wolfe/Tony Stone Images: 6
James P. Rowan/Tony Stone Images: 20
Leonard Lee Rue III/Tony Stone Images: 19
Norbert Wu/Tony Stone Images: cover
P. Harrison/Tony Stone Images: 15

On the cover...

Front cover: A walkingstick walks across a leaf at night.
Page 2: A *northern walkingstick* walks on a flower.

Table of Contents

Chapter	Page
Meet the Walkingstick	7
Are Walkingsticks Insects?	8
What is Camouflage?	11
How Big Are Walkingsticks?	12
How Do Walkingsticks Move Around?	14
What Do Walkingsticks Look Like?	17
Do Walkingsticks Have Enemies?	18
What is Another Means of Protection?	21
What Do Walkingsticks Eat?	22
How Are Baby Walkingsticks Born?	25
What Do Baby Walkingsticks Look Like?	27
What Is One Kind Of Special Feature?	28
Index & Glossary	32

Imagine that it's almost nighttime, and you are walking through a forest. Just as you reach a big tree, you see a hungry bird land on a branch. It is looking for some tasty bugs. The bird looks and looks, but it can't find anything to eat. Finally, the bird flies off to another part of the forest to find its dinner. As you watch, a stick begins to move, right where the bird was sitting. You rub your eyes and look again. The stick is not only moving, it's eating a leaf! What kind of creature are you looking at? It's a walkingstick!

This walkingstick is walking up a tree.

Are Walkingsticks Insects?

The walkingstick is a kind of **insect**. An insect is an animal with three separate body parts. Insects have a head, a chest (called a **thorax**), and a stomach (called an **abdomen**). Like most insects, walkingsticks also have six legs. Most insects have two pairs of wings, but walkingsticks don't have any wings at all.

This *northern walkingstick* is standing in a defensive position.

Walkingsticks look strange, but the shape of their bodies is very important. They look like small tree branches. Walkingsticks are very hard to see! This kind of hiding is called **camouflage**. Camouflage helps an animal hide from its enemies. It makes the animal look like a plant or a rock.

The walkingstick's long, thin, bumpy body looks like a little twig. The body even changes color to match the trees. In the spring, when the branches and leaves are green, the walkingstick is green. In the fall, when the branches and leaves turn brown, the walkingstick turns brown, too!

Tropical walkingsticks like this one look like branches.

How Big Are Walkingsticks?

Most walkingsticks that live in the United States are about three inches long. One kind can grow to be over a foot long! It is called the *Asian walkingstick*. The Asian walkingstick is the longest insect in the world.

This northern walkingstick is about four inches long.

How Do Walkingsticks Move Around?

Walkingsticks move only at night. They have small eyes and very long feelers, called **antennae**. To make themselves look even more like branches, walkingsticks also have six long, skinny legs. These long legs help the insect hide, but they aren't very good for walking. Because the walkingstick can't move very well, it stands still all day long. When night comes, it starts to move around—but not very far! Walkingsticks usually move just far enough to eat the leaves they have watched all day.

This northern walkingstick is sitting very still on a tree trunk.

What Do Walkingsticks Look Like?

Walkingsticks look different depending on where they live. Walkingsticks that live in the eastern and the southern United States all look like small twigs and branches. Those that live in jungles are much bigger. They also have sharp spines that look like thorns. In China and the Far East, walkingsticks have flatter legs and bodies. They look like the flat leaves of the trees that grow there.

One of the strangest walkingsticks of all is small, thin and stays green all the time. It makes its home on the ground. This walkingstick camouflages itself by standing up—it looks just like a blade of grass!

This beautiful *moving leaf* looks like the leaves around it.

Do Walkingsticks Have Enemies?

Even though walkingsticks are hard to see, they still have many enemies. More than fifteen different types of birds like to eat walkingsticks—if they can find them. And even if a walkingstick can escape the birds, it is still in danger. Lizards and mice like to eat walkingsticks, too. Animals that eat other animals are called **predators**.

This walkingstick is very hard to see next to the tree's bark.

What is Another Means of Protection?

Besides camouflage, some walkingsticks have another trick to help them escape from predators. If they feel a touch or get scared, they just tuck up their legs and fall to the ground! The predator thinks the walkingstick is dead. The walkingstick lies on the ground and stays still until the predator leaves. Once the danger is gone, it gets up and slowly climbs the tree again.

This walkingstick is sitting on some leaves.

What Do Walkingsticks Eat?

Walkingsticks are plant-eaters. At night, they move around their tree, eating leaves. If many walkingsticks live in the same tree, the leaves disappear quickly!

Walkingsticks don't bite or sting or harm people. But if a lot of walkingsticks live in fruit trees, they can cause a great deal of damage. Then people think they are a nuisance.

This walkingstick is looking for leaves to eat.

How Are Baby Walkingsticks Born?

At the end of the summer, female walkingsticks lay their eggs. The eggs are hard, shiny, black and look like little seeds. The females lay the eggs while they are still high up in the trees. Each egg must drop all the way down to the ground. That can be a long way! If a lot of female walkingsticks live in one tree, it looks and sounds as if it is raining eggs.

When the first frosts of winter come, the adult walkingsticks die. But the eggs survive on the ground all winter. Their hard shells protect them. In the spring the eggs hatch and the baby walkingsticks are born.

Walkingstick eggs are black and shiny.

What Do Baby Walkingsticks Look Like?

A baby walkingstick looks like a little adult. It spends all spring and summer growing. Young walkingsticks don't grow the same way people do, because they have a hard, shell-like skin. When they get too big for their old skin, they shed it, or **molt**. There is always a new, bigger skin underneath. A walkingstick molts up to six times before it becomes an adult.

This adult walkingstick has its final skin.

What Is One Kind of Special Feature?

Because baby walkingsticks are young and slow, birds like to attack them. But the babies are able to do something very special if they get hurt. Sometimes a young walkingstick loses a leg or an antenna during an attack. If it does, it just grows a new one! The new body part appears the next time the walkingstick molts.

This walkingstick is fully grown.

Walkingsticks like cherry or oak trees best, but they live in almost any forest. There might be lots of them, but they are very hard to see! That's because they hide so well. The next time you are walking through the forest, look closely at the branches of a tree. If you are very, very lucky, one of those twigs might just turn out to be a walkingstick!

This hungry walkingstick is looking for leaves to eat.

Glossary

abdomen (AB-duh-men)
The abdomen is the stomach area of an insect.

antennae (an-TEH-nee)
Long feelers on an insect's head that help it to know what is around are called antennae.

camouflage (KAM-uh-flazh)
When an animal uses camouflage, it can hide from its enemies by looking just like the plants or rocks that it is sitting next to. The walkingstick has camouflage to make it look like a branch.

insect (IN-sekt)
Animals that have a body divided into three parts are insects.

thorax (THOR-ax)
The thorax is the chest of an insect.

molt (MOLT)
To shed the outer layer of the skin. Dragonflies molt as they grow.

predator (PRED-uh-ter)
An animal that hunts and eats other animals is called a predator. Birds, lizards and rodents are all predators that hunt the walkingstick.

Index

insects, 8

babies, 25, 27

body, 8, 11, 14, 17

camouflage, 11, 14

enemies, 18

food, 22

location, 31

movement, 14

protection, 21

size, 12

skin, 27